PERSONAL CREDIT DIARY

A Path to Good Credit and
   Maintaining Good a Credit rating

By Ella Butcher

ELLA BUTCHER
PHILADELPHIA, PENNSYLVANIA

TABLE OF CONTENTS

INTRODUCTION 5

FICO SCORE INFORMATION 7

THINGS TO DO 9

SCORING 10

CREDIT MONITORING 11

HOW TO READ A CREDIT REPORT 12

SAMPLE CREDIT REPORT 13

HELP INFORMATION 14

BILL MONITORING 17

HOUSEHOLD BUDGET 32

BILL CALENDAR 33

DREAM BOARD INFOMATION 34

CREDIT NOTES 36

PERSONAL INFORMATION 60

CERTIFICATE 64

Introduction

What's more frustrating than being turned down for any type of credit, due to a bad credit file, knowing you can afford it.

Consumers in our country have or have had some type of credit. You can choose to accept or reject credit. However , people in our society are   practically forced to obtain credit due to various reasons. Understanding how credit works is powerful! Whatever you get …. Get understanding. Remember; always research information.

Individuals are now facing a higher credit deficit than ever. Without credit, our country would encounter a greater recession. How long are you going to continue sowing a good credit seed into bad credit soil and then you say… "My credit is bad I need a higher score." With bad credit, you are constantly in a war with credit consultants, bill collectors, attorneys, creditors, foreclosures and the legal system. With this diary, you will understand credit, learn how to maintain a good credit rating, how to get higher credit score, how to manage your bills, and how to deal with all types of credit obstacles, that may come your way.

The C's to Good Credit.

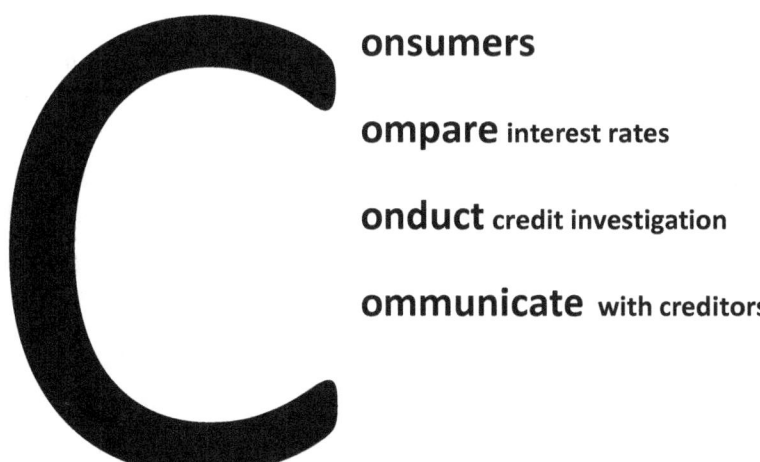

C **onsumers**

ompare interest rates

onduct credit investigation

ommunicate with creditors

Indemnification

You agree to indemnify, defend and hold harmless Ella Butcher and its affiliates, and their respective officers, directors, employees, agents, licensors and suppliers, and any third party providers of information or services to credit information, from and against all losses, expenses, damages and costs, including reasonable attorneys' fees, resulting from your violation of this education diary or any Customer Agreement applicable to products you have obtained.

Information and products offered by Ella Butcher through this are provided "as is" and without any express or implied warranty or representation of any kind, including warranties of merchantability for a particular purpose, or non-infringement. Ella Butcher makes no representation concerning, nor does it warrant or guaranty the correctness, comprehensiveness, completeness, accuracy, timeliness, merchantability, or fitness for any particular use or purpose of any information, products, or services offered by Ella Butcher and others through this Credit Diary.

In no event will Ella Butcher be liable to any party for any damages of any kind, including but not limited to direct, indirect, special or consequential damages, for any use of this Diary or any linked information including, without limitation, lost profits, loss of use, business interruption, loss of programs or other data, or failure to achieve any particular result, whether in an action based on contract, negligence, other tort, or strict liability, even if Ella Butcher is expressly advised of the possibility of those types of damages. Some jurisdictions do not allow the exclusion or limitation of warranties or damages in certain types of agreements, so the above exclusions or limitations may not apply to you.

Information in this Credit Diary is gathered from various web sites, books, and other individuals experiences for educational purposes with granted permission. In doing so, this credit dairy will help those with no or little time to perform their own credit research.

THE PERSONAL CREDIT DIARY. COPYRIGHT © 2009 by Ella Butcher. All rights reserved.

This diary may not be reproduced in whole or in part, by mimeograph or any other means, without permission.

For more information contact us at www.personalcreditdiary.org

ISBN - 978-0-983-42660-8

Printed in the United States *of* America

PERSONAL CREDIT DIARY

Understanding you Credit Score

What is Credit?
Whenever you make a purchase today with the promise to pay for it tomorrow, you are using credit. Having credit lets you make purchases when you don't have cash. available. Before a lender will allow you to use credit, they must first believe that you can be trusted to repay the amount of credit you use. This is considered financial trustworthiness.

What's in a Credit Report?
-Identifying Information
-Trade Lines (credit accounts)
-Credit Inquirer
-Public Records and collections

Type of Credit
Number of prevalence and recent information on various types of accounts (credit cards, retail accounts, installment loans, mortgage, and consumer finance accounts).

Things That Can Hurt Your Score
- Paying late
- Not paying at all
- Having an account sent to collections.
- Defaulting on a loan
- Charged Off
- Filing bankruptcy
- Having your home foreclosed
- Getting a judgment
- High credit card balances
- Maxed out credit cards

What's in Your FICO Scores?
FICO Scores are calculated from a lot of different credit data in your credit report. This data can be grouped into five categories as outlined above. The percentages in the chart reflect how important each of the categories is in determining your FICO score.

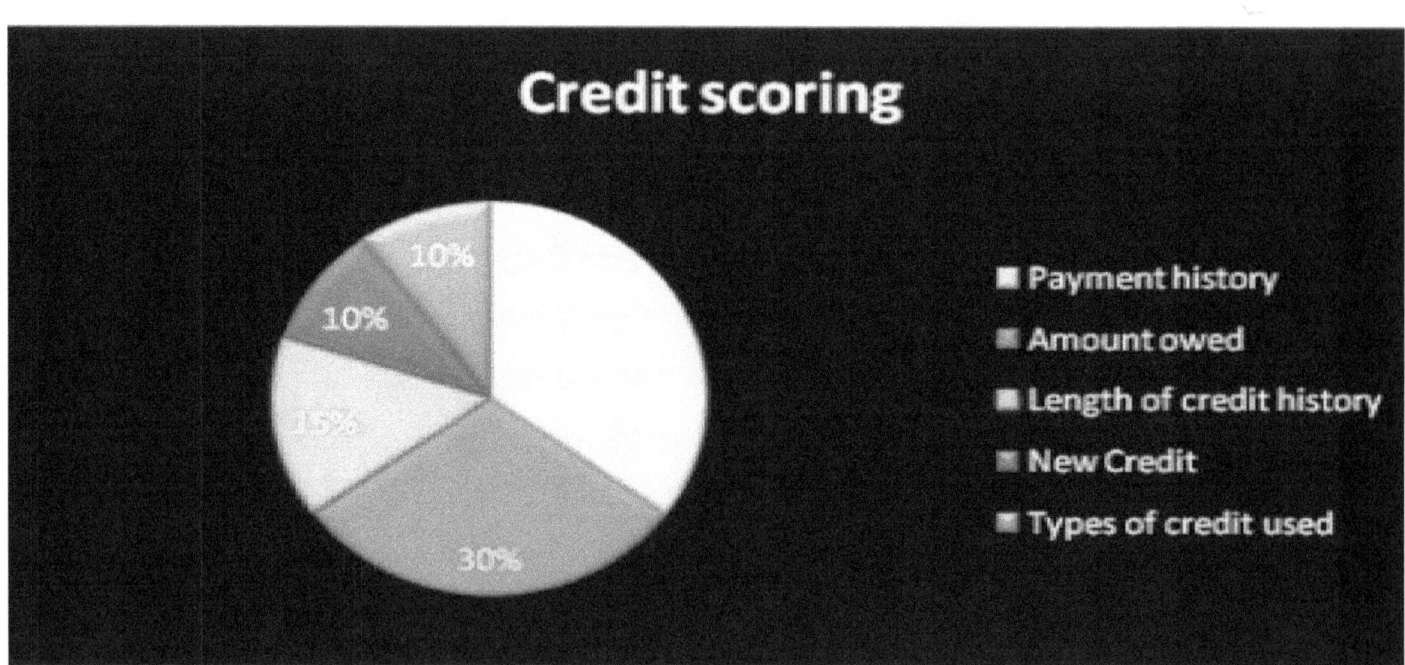

How is my score calculated?

1. Payment History impacts your credit **35%**. Meaning any latest; collections; charge offs; bankruptcies; judgments; liens or the like will hurt the score. All is time based, the older the information the less it is contributing to the scores.

2. Utilization impacts your credit **30%**. It is best to have several accounts with low balances distributed then it is to have fewer accounts maxed out. To figure utilization: Balance (divided) by Credit Limit = percentage. Lower than 10% recommended per account, this is one of the fastest means for increasing the over all credit score.

3. Established History impacts your credit **15%**. The longer you maintain open accounts with creditors the better. When first starting out of course this is not easy; but this is where getting added as an Authorized User to another persons established credit comes in best. Remember that the contributor must have an account that has long history; clean payment record; high credit limit; and low balance. Also need to check with the creditor to insure that they have a policy to report authorized user accounts to all three major credit reporting agencies.

Note: Authorized user accounts are the best way to go; since you are not legally responsible for the debt rather than Joint or Co-Signer accounts. Also, if this account starts to report negatively; these accounts are usually easier to remove from the credit reports by either contacting the creditor and requesting termination of the relationship; or disputing through the Credit Reporting ACT.

4. Inquiries impacts your credit **10%**. Don't apply for credit unless you know you can get it or that you need to get it; unnecessary credit inquiries are going to hurt the scores - especially if your over all credit file is small to begin with.

Tips: When applying for credit pull your own credit report first (this is a soft hit and will not drop your score). With your credit report in hand go visit your local banks or credit unions. Show them the reports; and do not allow them to pull your credit report if they decline you. If they say yes, you are approved, and then they will need to pull credit report to seal the deal. Mortgage & Auto industry has special rules for inquiries: all applications for credit resulting in pulled credit reports within a 14-day period will only count as one inquiry & will be suppressed from affecting credit scores for 30 days. If you plan to go shopping for a mortgage or a car, do your research before choosing a bank, so that the scores are not affected too much.

5. Mix of Credit **10%**. Use different types of credit (revolving; installment; auto; mortgage...) evenly.

Also remember the advice which a lender gives you is productive for getting a loan; but not always good for the credit scores. If they tell you to consolidate and close accounts, be careful how you go about this, most people's compliance usually results in dropped credit scores. You are shrinking your overall available credit limit verses your balances... so remember you do not want to hurt the utilization by consolidating and closing accounts behind you.

What is the range of FICO scores?

FICO Classic or BEACON scores can range from 300 to 850, but the majority of scores fall within the 600s and 800s.
Note: Scores higher than 720-750+ is ideal. Once you get this high, you have excellent score regardless.

What information is NOT used in calculating my FICO score?

1. Your race, color, religion, national origin, sex or marital status

2. Your age

3. Your salary, occupation, title, employer, date employed or employment history

4. Where you live

5. Certain types of inquiries such as promotional, account review, insurance or employment related inquiries

6. Any information not found in your credit file

7. Any information that is not proven to be a predictive of future credit performance

How often does my score change?

Your credit file is continually updated with new information from your creditors. The FICO score is calculated based on the latest information contained in your file at the time the score is requested. Therefore, your FICO score from a month ago is probably not the same score a lender would get from the credit-reporting agency today. The reason some creditors tell you it can take up to 90 days for a correction account to be updated in your credit file. **Is because some creditors only report quarterly** and others report the 1st of every month.

Why are my scores different?

Your scores may be different at each of the three main credit-reporting agencies as the FICO score only considers the data in your credit file from that agency. If your score from the three credit reporting agencies is different, it is probably
Because some information the agencies have are different. (some creditors don't report to all agencies). Also, keep in mind that there is a different FICO formula for each credit-reporting agency.

How can I improve my score?

It takes time, you didn't damage your credit overnight and you can't it fix over night so **be patient.** Scores reflect credit payment patterns over time with more priority on recent information. The best advice is to manage your credit responsibly over time.

Scores automatically improve, as one's overall credit picture gets better. That means showing a historical pattern of paying your bills on time and using credit conservatively.

Things to DO:

1. Pay your bills on time. Delinquent payments and collections can have a major negative impacts on your score.

2. If you have been paying late and missed payments, get current and stay current. The longer you pay your bills on time, the better your score.

3. If you are having trouble making ends meet, contact your creditors or see a credit counselor. This will not improve your score immediately, but if you can begin to manage your credit and pay on time, your score will get better over time.

4. Keep balances low on credit cards and other revolving credit. High outstanding debt can affect a score.

5. Pay off debt rather than transferring your balance to other cards.

6. Re-establish your credit history if you have had problems in the passed.

7. Opening new accounts (not rapidly) paying them off in full will raise your score.

8. It is OK to request and check your own credit file. This will not affect your score, as long as you order your credit file directly from the credit-reporting agency (Trans Union, Experian, Equifax) or through an organization authorized to provide credit files to consumers

9. Apply for and open new credit accounts only as needed. Because, every time you open a new account it can lower score.

Things not to DO:

1. Close unused credit cards as a short-term strategy to raise your score. **NEVER** close an open account with a balance! Closing an account with a balance will lower your score.

2. Do not open new accounts to increase your credit score, because new accounts are known to lower credit scores.

3. If you have been managing your credit for a short time, do not open many new accounts too rapidly. New accounts will lower your average account age, which will have a larger effect on your score ,if you do not have a lot of other credit information. Also, rapid account build-up can look risky if you are a new credit user. Do your rate shopping for a given loan within a focused period. FICO scores distinguish between a search for a single loan and a search for many new credit lines, in part by the length of time over which inquiries occur.

If derogatory information is removed, will my score increase?

It depends. It is impossible to say how important any single factor or new information is in determining your score because the importance of each factor depends on the overall information in your credit report. What is important in scoring is the mix of information, which varies from person to person and for any one person over time.

For some people, a given factor may be more important than for someone else with a different credit history. In addition, as the information in your credit report changes, so does the importance of any factor in determining your score. Some helpful tips are:

1. If there is inaccurate derogatory information on your credit report, get it corrected.

2. The score evaluates derogatory information in several ways - how often, how recent and how severe. If you have a pattern (e.g. several
derogatory items and late payments) of this type of behavior, removing one of these may not affect the score very much.

Be aware that:

1. Paying off a collection account, late pay or derogatory item will not remove it from your credit file (It just satisfies the debt). It will stay on your file for seven years along with any dollar amount associated with the past due.

2. Closing an account does not remove it from your credit file. A closed account will still show up on your credit file and may be considered in calculating your score.

How long will a derogatory stay on my reports?

In general. The 7-year period referred to date of late activity not date opened. Charged off to profit and loss, or subjected to any similar action, upon the expiration of the 180-day period beginning on the date of the delinquency which immediately preceded the collection activity, charge off to profit and loss, or similar action.

In legalese, that means that an account reports 7 years from the date it goes bad, period. Paying shouldn't reset it. Monitor your credit regularly, because some collection agencies will report the account as if it was a current delinquent, not the accurate date of last activity. **No derogatory information was reported on my file, why did I receive a reason code relating to derogatory data?**
Delinquency or serious delinquency may raise a red flag on any accounts that are currently delinquent, as well as on any accounts that are currently in good standing but may indicate historical delinquency in the past e.g. going into collection status. Evidence of current or historical delinquency may appear in the following fields

The "Account Status" of the account (e.g. 30 or more days past due, chapter 13, repossession, bad debt, placed for collection, foreclosure, included in bankruptcy, etc.).

2. An indication of any "Past Due" amount.

3. The "Times Past Due" and "Previous High Status" of the account or other historical payment indicators showing previous 30, 60, 90, or 120 days delinquent status on the account, or previous derogatory status, and when it occurred.

4. Counters indicating the number of times an account has been "30 Days", "60 Days", "90 Days" or "120 Days" past due during the life
of the account.

Credit Monitoring

Credit Monitoring helps maintain and alerts you with any changes in your credit file.

Items included in a Credit Monitoring Program

- Weekly monitoring of 400 data sources for new information tied to your identity,
- Quarterly FICO® credit score and report monitoring
- New names
- New dates of birth
- New social security numbers
- New addresses
- New phone numbers
- Quarterly TransUnion credit report analysis, monitoring:
- Changes to your TransUnion FICO® score, and reasons for changes
- Changes to name, date of birth, or social security number
- Newly listed addresses or phone numbers
- Newly listed employers
- Newly opened accounts
- Recent applications for new credit
- Recent increases in account balances
- Accounts in bad status
- Newly listed public records, such as bankruptcies, foreclosures, and tax liens
- Newly listed collection company records
- 6 easy-to-understand charts that show changes in:
- TransUnion FICO® score
- Balance owed on all accounts
- Balance past due on all accounts
- Number of recent applications for credit
- Number of negative problems on credit report
- Number of accounts in bad status

Visit www.personalcreditdiary.com to sign up for credit monitoring.

Get your free credit report at www.annualcreditreport.com

How To Read A Credit Report?

A credit report commonly consists of several sectors: (1) personal information; (2) public record information; (3) collection agency account information; (4) credit account information; and (5) inquiries.

All of the sectors are easy to read and understand with the exclusive of two: the credit account information section and the inquiry section. This is because the credit bureaus use special coding to categorize and report type of account and payment history. Once you understand the key, it is easy to read these sections of your credit file.

Credit Account Information
Alongside each credit account in your file will be a letter designating your relationship to that account. Below is the key indicating what these letters mean:

J = Joint
I = Individual
U = Undesignated
A = Authorized User
T = Terminated
M = Maker
C = Co-maker or Co-signor
B = On behalf of another person
S = Shared

In addition to the above coding, you will also find special coding used to record the type of account and your payment history. Below is the key indicating what these letters and numbers mean:

O = Open (entire balance due each month)
R = Revolving (amount due can change each month)
I = Installment (fixed amount due each month)
0 = Approved, but account is too new to rate or not yet used
1 = Paid as agreed
2 = 30 or more days past due
3 = 60 or more days past due
4 = 90 or more days past due
5 = 120 or more days past due or is a collection account
7 = Making regular payments under a wage earner plan or other arrangement
8 = Repossession
9 = Charged off account

Therefore, based on the above, you could quickly go down the relevant column in your credit file and the following alphanumeric combinations would be indications you have an excellent payment history: O1, R1 or I1. Of course, you don't want to find anything that ends in 2, 3, 4, 5, 7, 8 or 9.

Date Opened - This is the month and year you opened the account with the credit grantor.

Months Reviewed - Lists the number of months the account history has been reported.

Last Activity - Indicates the date of the last activity on the account. This may be the date of your last payment or last charge.

SAMPLE CREDIT REPORT

DATE: 02-23-2009   TIME:11:48:25   SUBJECT ID:

STATE ISSUED-PA

PERSONAL REDIT INFORMATION SERVICES,
*CONSUMER,JOHN,Q,JR,JANE   SINCE 03/10/73 FAD 01/31/94
 9412,PAUL,ST,PHILADELPHIA,PA,19154,TPE RPTD 07/86
            TELEPHONE NUMBER (215)555-1212 CRT 07/85
410,BROWN GROVE,DR,PHILA,PA,19119,CRT RPTD 06/85
    *****ALSO KNOWN AS CCONSUMER,JR*****

BDS-03/03/49, SSS-900-00-0000 SSN VER: N
01 ES-ENGINEER,LOCKHEED,PHILA,PA,EMP 06/87,VER 03/92
02 EF-ENGINEER,CENTRAL POWER,ABINGTON,PA,,,,LEFT 05/87

****** PUBLIC RECORDS OR OTHER INFORMATION ******
05 04/92 BKRPT 401VF77, BP56789BP98,LIAB$98765,ASSET$7890, INDIVID, PERSONAL,VO
      L CH-7

****

****** COLLECTION ITEMS ******
LIST RPTD AMT/BAL DLA/ECOA AGENCY/CLIENT   STATUS/SERIAL
11/95 11/95 $1234567 11/95 401YC157   STAT UNKNOWN
       $1234567   I   DR SMITH   77755543326568T67
****
FIRM/IDENT   CODE CS RPTD LIMIT HICR BAL $ DLA MR(30-60-90+)MAX/DE
ECOA/ACCOUNT   NUMBER   OPND P/DUE TERM   24 MONTH HISTORY

FIRSTAR   636BB3150 R0 01/00 500 ◄top date when account closed
I/OIU9099   09/88 --- ◄bottom date when account opened

HFC UNSEC 832FP1018 R5 01/00 1900 ---
I/AQ0009876   09/88 --- ---
ACCOUNT CLOSED BY CREDIT GRANTOR

GTE MOBLN 645ZZ9149 R1 10/99 900 ---
I/ZXCV5   09/88 --- ---

GTE MOBLN 645ZZ9149 R1 08/98 900 ---
I/Z3534   09/88 --- ---

VLLY FORD 613AN1557 I2 08/98 900 ---
I/Y23345   09/88 --- ---

GRAND TOTALS

INQUIRIES
*INQS-ADBUSCOMP 999ZZ49098 02/23/00   ◄Name of the Company and date the credit was odered
    CBA MTG DV 869ZBOO189 02/22/00
    ADBUSCOMP 999ZZ49098 02/22/00

CONSUMER STATEMENT
Date of report 02/14/2009

Helpful Information

WWW.Equal Credit Opportunity Act
WWW.U.S Government Identity Theft Web Site
WWW.Identity Theft Complaint Form
WWW.FirstGov for Consumers
WWW. The National "Do Not Call" Registry
WWW.Federal Trade Commission
WWW.FTC Consumer Complaint Form
WWW.Attorney General
WWW.Transunion.com
WW.Experian.com
WWW.Equifax.com

Inquiries concern

Inquiries that impacts your FICO score

The type of credit inquiry that impact your FICO score. When you apply for a mortgage, auto loan or other credit, you authorize the lender to request a copy of your credit report. These types of inquiries, prompted by your own actions, appear on your credit report and are included in your FICO score

Inquiries that don't impact your FICO score
Your own credit report requests, credit checks made by businesses to offer you goods or services, or inquiries made by businesses with whom you already have a credit account do not count toward your FICO score. Credit checks by prospective employers also do not count. These types of inquiries may appear on your credit report, but they are not included in your FICO score. Inquiries can remain on your report up to 2 years.

Credit Q&A

What are some other examples of what lenders are doing to limit their risk, and what can I do to adjust to this "credit crisis " so that I'll continue to have a good FICO score?

Some banks are lowering credit lines and closing accounts that have had little or no recent activity. These actions can hurt your score if they result in higher credit utilization (percentage of balance to credit limit); therefore, you're going to want to preserve your credit lines by keeping your credit card accounts open and using them frequently – while, at the same time, maintaining low balances.

Helpful Information

How to spend your money and strengthen your credit score at the same time

When a client decides to make a store purchase of any goods with cash, simply purchase the product with his/her credit card. Take the cash that was intended to be spent on the item, deposit it into a bank account for an online bill payment or one may put the cash into an envelope and pay the bill when it comes in. note: **Try to pay more than the minimum payment.** To help establish a credit history. when the credit card bill comes in, do not pay the bill off in one payment. spread your payments out as much as possible ! preferably 12 months! this will show lenders that you are an responsible consumer. By paying your bills online, this will help prevent late payments. note: be sure to total your bills each month and make sure the monies are in your account before the due date.

How to help build a positive payment history and credit score using a financial institution

Open a bank account with a bank that offers secure loans with the lowest minimum cash requirement if possible. Two hundred dollars are normally the lowest cash requirement when getting an secure loan this loan is called "secure" because your loan is protected by your monies, that you currently have in your bank account. when you obtain the loan, do not spend the cash. Simply let the loan pay for it self by allowing the cash to remain in your bank account until the loan is paid in full ! With this loan, you do not need good credit or a high credit score. Note: You must have enough money in you account to cover the loan amount and the interest charge. PAYING off the loan in 12 months will help establish a positive payment history and improve your credit score! Once the loan is paid in full, simply repeat the process with another bank. **Remember: what one bank will not do, others that will!**

Note: It's not mandatory for creditors to report to the credit bureaus, its optional. Credit Bureaus are paid by the Creditors to report on your file. Also, some creditors only report to one out of several bureaus.

Credit Disability Insurance

Obtain disability insurance on all your credit cards, personal loans, auto loan (including extra disability insurance through your insurance agency in case you are injury in a car OR ANY accidents). Disability insurance will only cost you a few dollars more (**IT'S WORTH IT WHEN YOU ARE UNABLE TO MAKE YOUR PAYMENTS, AT LEAST YOUR BILLS WILL BE PAID**).

Please take your credit seriously…. It's very…very important!

Helpful Information

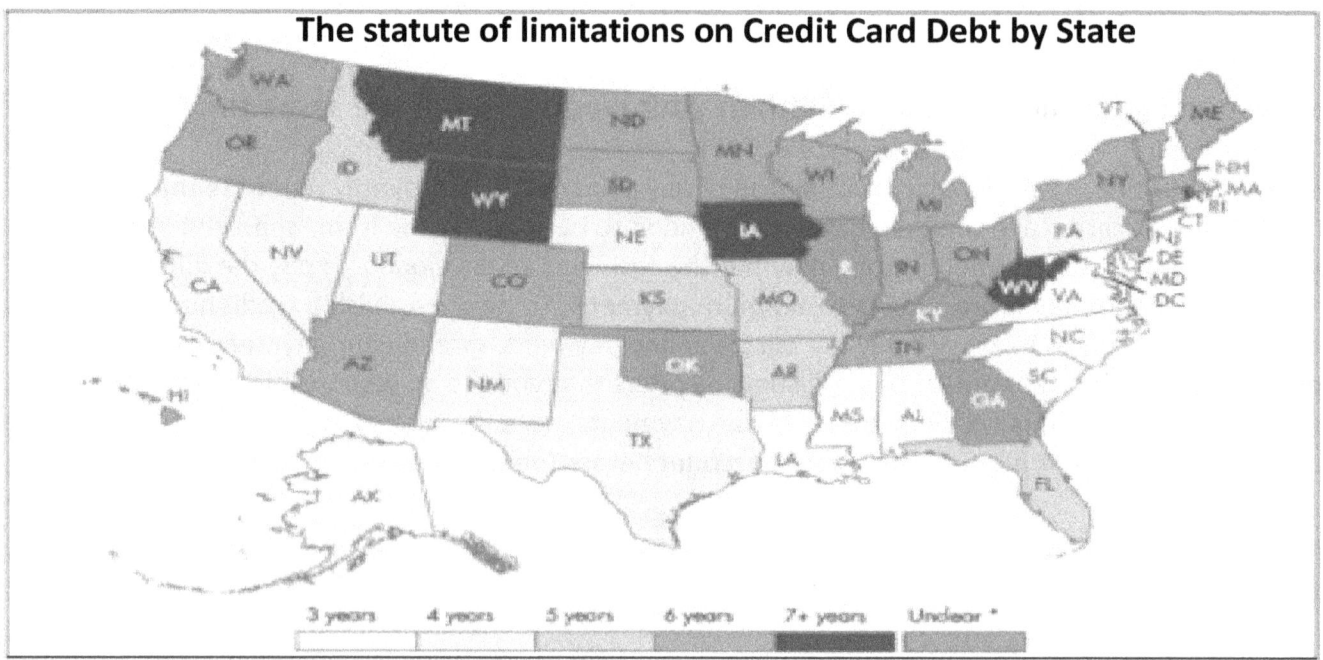

The legal meaning for statute of limitations is: ***THE TIME OF COMMENCING ACTIONS**-Time allowed that litigation-lawsuit can be brought.* (**See complete legal meaning of Statute of Limitations**). After that time, it has expired. Statute is a law. Passed by legislation and varies by state. The original **statute of limitations** begins at the onset of the contract signing (see more below for time barred debts). **Statute of limitations vary from state to state** but it is usually 4-6 years depending on the state. The term **statute of limitations** means the time allotted to legally enforce the debt. If a statute expires and someone sues you, it is up to you to bring the expired SOL defense. **Don't assume an expired statute of limitations means the other party is barred from attempting to collect**. It simply means that your defense is the expired SOL - not to enforce the lawsuit. The statute of limitations for your credit reports is separate. Items on your credit reports are seven years.

Are there separate SOL's for debts & credit reporting?
Many **people** confuse the statute of limitations to collect a debt with the time a debt is **allowed to remain on your credit reports.** The two are separate. Credit bureaus are allowed a certain time frame to report debts. **See reporting time for details.** Another big fear is that paying it will extend the time it is allowed to be reported on your credit. Debts are reported from FIRST delinquency or written off date, not by last activity or last payment. Exclusions would be tax liens, they remain from date paid for 7 years and can remain indefinitely if unpaid. Paying a debt will not restart the clock for reporting it but you could restart the clock for collecting it, so if you pay it, **either pay it in full or restrictively, as to have no worries. A promise to pay or partial payment can renew the statute in many states (you need to read your own state's rule** to know for sure), many people think that only a renewed promise to pay does this. That is not the case. Either or can renew the statute

What would you change to prevent credit problems in the future?

1._____

2._____

3._____

4._____

5._____

6._____

7._____

8._____

9._____

10._____

Bill Budget

Log down the amount and date when a bill is paid monthly.

	Bill	Amount	Date paid
1.	Visa Acct	$60.00	01/09/2009

2. _____

3. _____

4. _____

5. _____

6. _____

7. _____

8. _____

9. _____

10. _____

Bill Budget

Log down the amount and date when a bill is paid.

	Bill	Amount	Date paid
1.	Visa Acct	$60.00	02/09/2009

2. _____

3. _____

4. _____

5. _____

6. _____

7. _____

8. _____

9. _____

10. _____

Bill Budget

Log down the amount and date when a bill is paid.

	Bill	Amount	Date paid
1.	Visa Acct	$60.00	03/09/2009
2.			
3.			
4.			
5.			
6.			
7.			
8.			
9.			
10.			

Bill Budget

Log down the amount and date when a bill is paid.

	Bill	Amount	Date paid
1.	Visa Acct	$60.00	04/09/2009
2.			
3.			
4.			
5.			
6.			
7.			
8.			
9.			
10.			

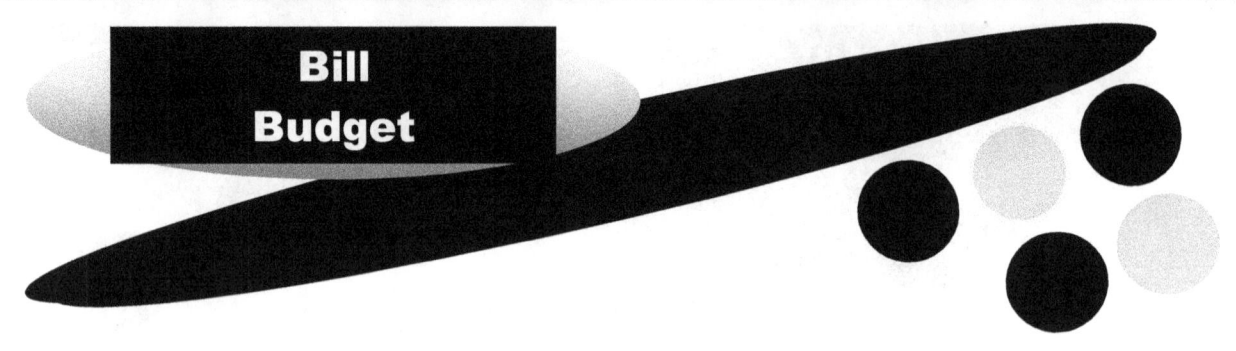

Bill Budget

Log down the amount and date when a bill is paid.

	Bill	Amount	Date paid
1.	Visa Acct	$60.00	05/09/2009
2.			
3.			
4.			
5.			
6.			
7.			
8.			
9.			
10.			

Bill Budget

Log down the amount and date when a bill is paid.

	Bill	Amount	Date paid
1.	Visa Acct	$60.00	06/09/2009

2. _____

3. _____

4. _____

5. _____

6. _____

7. _____

8. _____

9. _____

10. _____

Bill Budget

Log down the amount and date when a bill is paid.

Bill	Amount	Date paid
1. Visa Acct	$60.00	07/09/2009
2.		
3.		
4.		
5.		
6.		
7.		
8.		
9.		
10.		

Bill Budget

Log down the amount and date when a bill is paid.

	Bill	Amount	Date paid
1.	Visa Acct	$60.00	08/09/2009
2.			
3.			
4.			
5.			
6.			
7.			
8.			
9.			
10.			

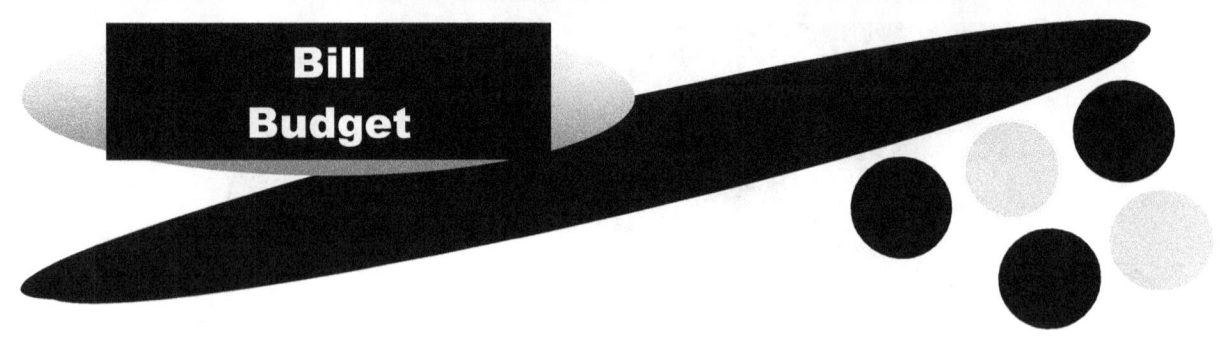

Bill Budget

Log down the amount and date when a bill is paid.

	Bill	Amount	Date paid
1.	Visa Acct	$60.00	09/09/2009
2.			
3.			
4.			
5.			
6.			
7.			
8.			
9.			
10.			

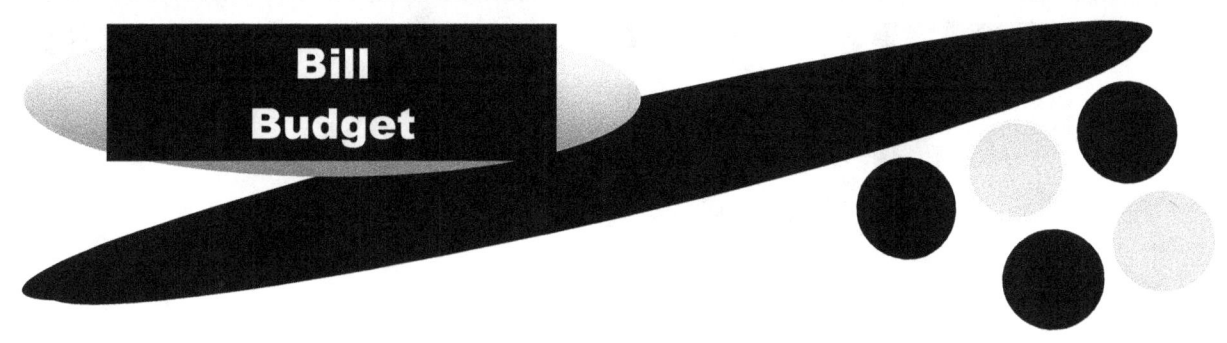

Bill Budget

Log down the amount and date when a bill is paid.

	Bill	Amount	Date paid
1.	Visa Acct	$60.00	10/09/2009
2.			
3.			
4.			
5.			
6.			
7.			
8.			
9.			
10.			

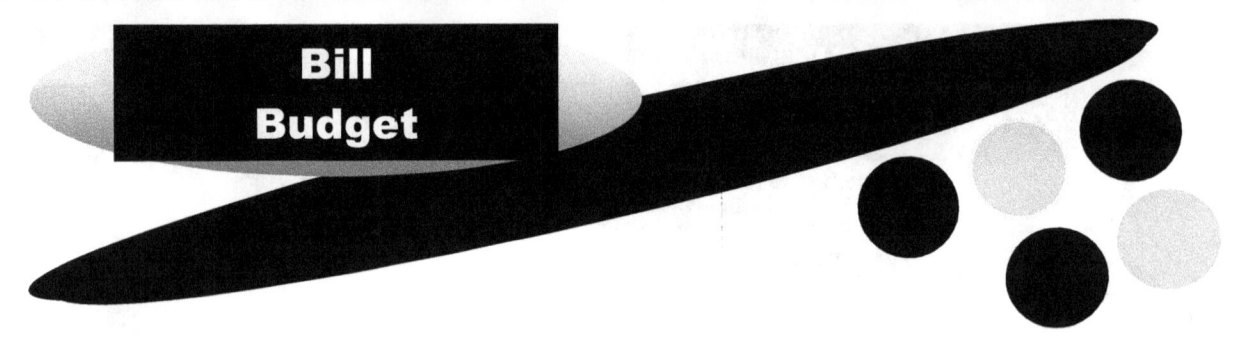

Bill Budget

Log down the amount and date when a bill is paid.

Bill	Amount	Date paid
1. Visa Acct	$60.00	11/09/2009

2. _____

3. _____

4. _____

5. _____

6. _____

7. _____

8. _____

9. _____

10. _____

Bill Budget

Log down the amount and date when a bill is paid.

Bill	Amount	Date paid
1. Visa Acct	$60.00	12/09/2009 |„
2.		
3.		
4.		
5.		
6.		
7.		
8.		
9.		
10.		

Bill Budget

Log down the amount and date when a bill is paid.

	Bill	Amount	Date paid
1.	Visa Acct	$60.00	01/09/2009
2.			
3.			
4.			
5.			
6.			
7.			
8.			
9.			
10.			

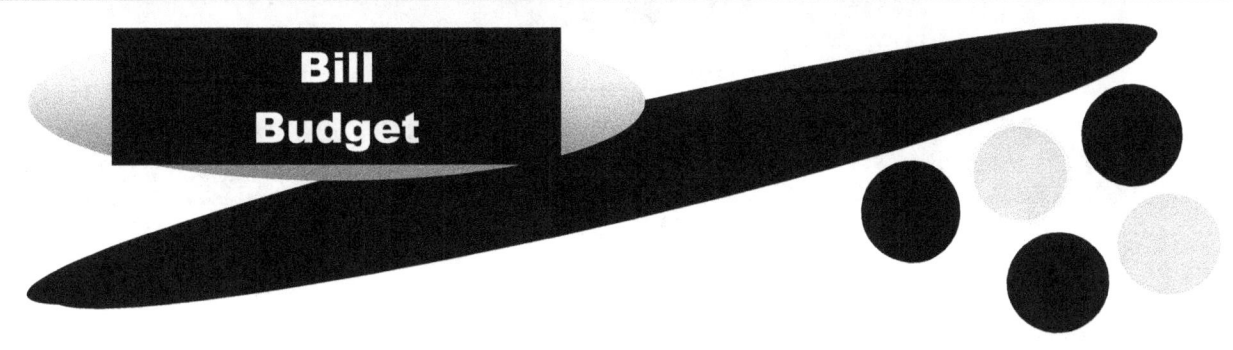

Bill Budget

Log down the amount and date when a bill is paid.

Bill	Amount	Date paid
1. Visa Acct	$60.00	01/09/2009
2.		
3.		
4.		
5.		
6.		
7.		
8.		
9.		
10.		

Household Budget

	Budget	Actual	Variance
Income			
Salary 1 (Take Home Pay)			$ -
Salary 2 (Take Home Pay)			-
<Other Income>	-		-
<Other Income>	-		-
Total Income	$ -		$ -
Expenses			
Fixed Costs			
Mortgage / Rent Expense			$ -
Car / Lease Payment(s)			-
Loan Payment(s)			-
Insurance - Car			-
Insurance - Homeowner's			-
Insurance - Life			-
Charitable Contributions			-
Childcare			-
<Other Fixed Cost>			-
<Other Fixed Cost>			-
Total Fixed Costs			$ -
Semi Variable Costs			
Electric / Gas Expense			$ -
Telephone Expense			-
Cable / Satellite Television Expense			-
Internet Expense			-
Food (Dining Out & Groceries)			-
Gasoline			-
Pet Supplies			-
Medical / Healthcare			-
Personal Care			-
<Other Semi Variable Costs>			-
<Other Semi Variable Costs>			-
Total Semi Variable Costs			$ -
Highly Variable Costs			
Entertainment			$ -
Gifts			-
Clothing			-
Miscellaneous			-
<Other Highly Variable Costs>			-
<Other Highly Variable Costs>			-
Total Highly Variable Costs			$ -
Total Expenses			$ -
Net Income			$ -

Bill Calendar

Write down your bills on the appropriate due date. Remove this page and place in a visible location. This is a monthly bill management tool.

Example

1	2	3	4	5	6	7
Mortgage $800.00						
8	9	10	11	12	13	14
					Gas bill $100.00	
15	16	17	18	19	20	21
Auto loan $500.00						
22	23	24	25	26	27	28
				Credit card $50.00		

Credit Dream Board

Create a **Personal Credit Dream Board** based on a one year goal
(meaning, if you had good credit, what could you accomplish in a year).

Dream Board Instructions

Step 1 : Decorate your poster board
Step 2 : Cut out pictures (example items listed below)
Step 3 : Attached each item on the board in the order you desire
Step 4 : Write comments next to each goal you would like to achieve (exp; paste a picture of a car on the board and write, my new car)
Step 5 : Cover your dream broad with plastic. Suggestion, take it to an office supply store to be professionally covered

Items needed to complete your Dream Board

- Poster board (erasable)
- School white glue, scotch tape, glitter & ribbons
- Newspapers & Magazines (for desired clippings)
- Your personal photos
- Books
- Markers, pen & crayons scissor
- 8 1/2 x 11 paper

Start your dream board with the list below or create your own list

Example: If I had good credit, I would….

- Buy a new car
- Buy my dream home
- Get a credit card with a low interest rate
- Start a business
- Pay off student loans
- Take a dream vacation
- Become an Investor
- Get a job (any job that's credit driven)
- Change my auto/homeowners insurance to get a better rate

Label your dream board with a starting date. Paste your dream list on the poster board from your personal list (design the board to your liken). Once completed, hang your board in a preferred area. You now have your first official **Personal Credit Dream Board.** This will help achieve your one year credit goal. Continue adding information as your dreams continue to change. Spend a few minutes in front of your board before you start your day! Make your board the last thing you read before going to sleep.

Credit Notes:

Credit Notes:

Credit Notes:

Credit Notes:

Credit Notes:

Credit Notes:

Credit Notes:

Credit Notes:

Credit Notes:

Credit Notes:

Credit Notes:

Credit Notes:

Credit Notes:

Credit Notes:

Credit Notes:

Credit Notes:

Credit Notes:

Credit Notes:

Credit Notes:

Credit Notes:

Credit Notes:

Credit Notes:

Credit Notes:

Credit Notes:

Personal Information

Name:_____

Address:_____

Date Diary started :_____

Date Diary ended :_____

Log down your credit scores at the beginning and finishing of your Diary:

	Beginning	**End**
Trans union	_____	_____
Experian	_____	_____
Equifax	_____	_____

Acknowledgement

I would like to thank those individuals who kindly gave me permission for the copyright material. Also, I would like to personally thank my editorial team.

A Word From The Author

Dear Friend:

I'm pleased you have taken the time out to read this special edition of the *"Personal Credit Diary"*. This literature will help you maintain and rebuild your credit worthiness.

This Diary is very special because it's at the heart of my vision to share this information with individuals that's taking their credit matters seriously. In doing so, this diary will help you to achieve your credit goals.

I hope you're inspired! Please enjoy your Personal Credit Diary.

Ella Butcher

P.S. I'm delighted to encourage you to share this information with others.

About the Author

For over fourteen years, Ms. Ella Butcher has been writing on and offering her services to the community of Greater Philadelphia. A life-long believer in the importance of financial literacy, Ms. Butcher offers mortgage and housing services through her own mortgage broker company, Butcher Investers, LLC, based out of Ms. Butcher's headquarters in Philadelphia Pennsylvania.

She delivers keynote speeches, workshops, seminars, and teaches the credit education course at Philadelphia Temple University's Pan-African Studies Community Education Program with the ability to move her audience to action. She has a message that will leave a lasting impact on her listeners well after message is render. She's the co-host on several local radio station discussing her book "Personal Credit Diary" and program on issues relevant to today's financial society. Ella can serve you or any organizations and businesses by delivering her message.

Also based out of Ms. Butcher's location in Philadelphia is Peaches and Cream, Inc., a 501(c)(3) nonprofit organization that provides youth services in the form of mentorship, academic tutoring, teen entrepreneurship, and after-school programs, among others. Ms. Butcher's dedication to providing services to and affecting change for under-resourced populations expands beyond Philadelphia: Ms. Butcher, among other political appointments, serves as the state's Executive Director of the Pennsylvania New Majority Council PAGOP, an organization aiming to increase minority participation in politics. Known to the community as a tireless, passionate force with an energy that is almost "magical," Ms. Butcher has dedicated her life to giving back to the city she has grown to call her home, offering financial, political, and youth-based services indispensible to the community at large.

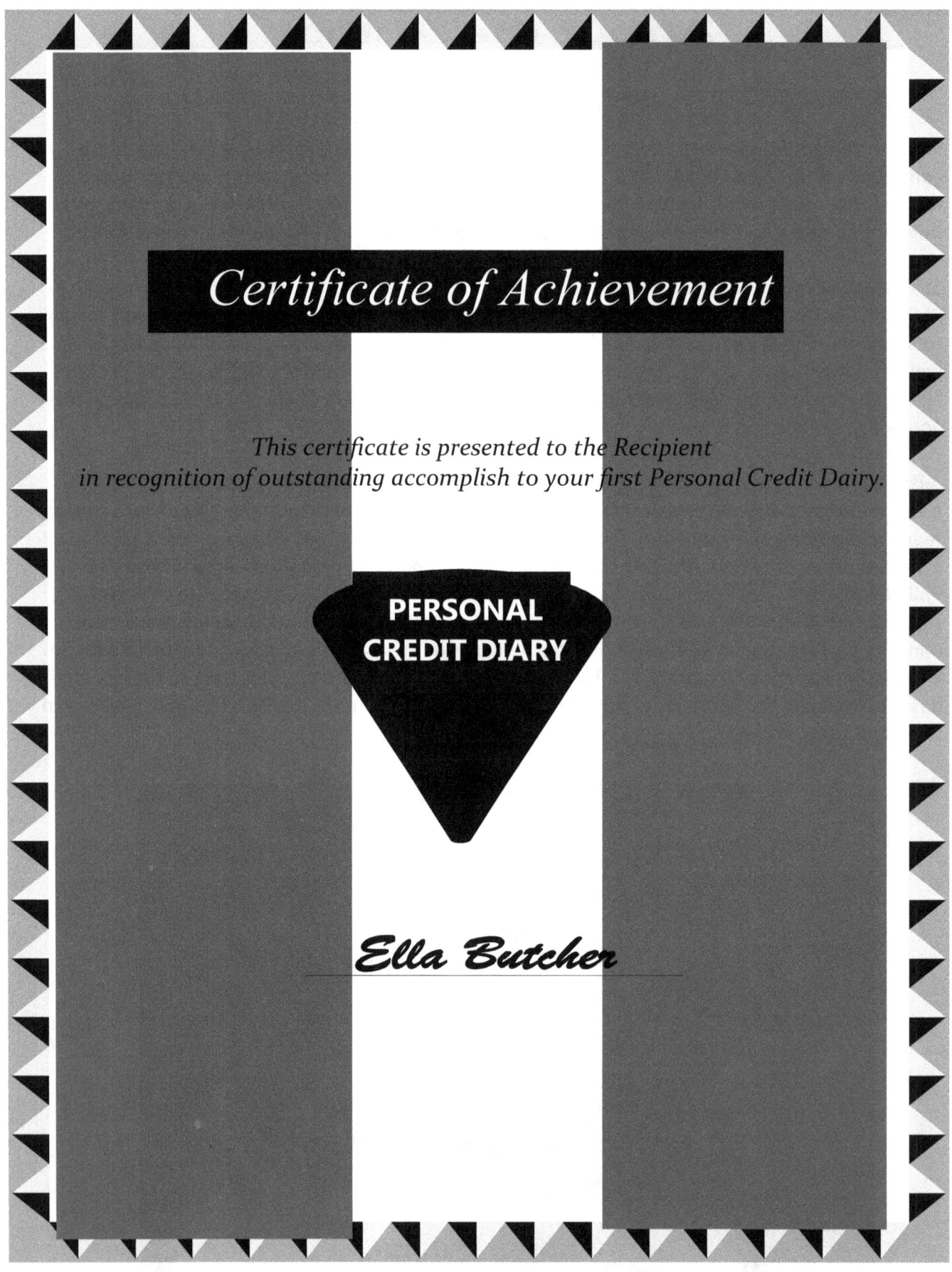

www.ingramcontent.com/pod-product-compliance
Lightning Source LLC
Chambersburg PA
CBHW081508040426
42446CB00017B/3439